The Women Widowed to Themselves

Copyright © 2015 by Lora Mathis
ISBN 978-1-329-38416-3

Second Edition-Copyright © 2015 by Lora Mathis
First Edition-Copyright © 2015 by Lora Mathis

Cover Copyright © 2015 Brianna Meli

All rights reserved. No part of this book may be reproduced in any form or by any electronic or mechanical means, including information storage and retrieval systems, without prior permission in writing from the publisher, except for brief quotations embodied in critical articles and review.

Published in Portland, OR
by Where Are You Press

For Robi and for you, if you need this.

CONTENTS

How I Want You To Read This Book..................8
Subtleties..................9
Heavy Blood..................10
Primal Desire..................11
You Like That Huh..................12
I Am Not The Sea..................14
Baby Darling Honey..................16
How To Disappear (And Never Be Found Again)..................18
Quiet Game Starting Now..................19
Take Your Time..................21
Today..................22
Reclusive..................23
Patter-Mouthed..................24
But I Thank You For The Poems You Gave Me..................26
You Know The Word Consent..................27
Look..................29
Is It Really My Fault..................30
An Offering..................33
Hand-Me-Down Rag..................34
The Dust On This Poem Could Choke You..................35
Your Type..................37
You Were An Illness I Barely Beat..................38
The Thought of You..................40
I Practice Death To Forget You..................41
Flank of Meat Cooked Up..................42
Make It Real..................43
Just So It's Clear..................44
Salt..................45
He Is A Song I Have Stuck In My Head..................47
Purity Is A Barbed-Wire Fence Shouting Keep Out..................48
Sex With You..................51
Put Pressure On A Wound To Stop It From Bleeding..................52
The Women Widowed to Themselves..................53
Trained Silence..................54
Can't Keep Up..................56
Birthday Cake..................57
An Apology To My Body..................58

Can You Taste The Self-Loathing In This Poem...................60
The Joy of Being Alive..61
How Can You Haunt Me If You're Still Here.....................62
It's Like A Poem I Keep Writing..................................63
As Soon As I Forget I Am Reminded Again......................64
Your Heart Is The Size of a Fist..................................65
Hot Sun Through My Jeans...66
I Sing The Song of Myself..67
Pulling Feathers..69
When Your Heart Breaks Get Up and Stomp On It.............71
Send This To Your Valentine......................................72
Made Up In Your Make-Up...73
The Slivered Walks..74
New Self Same City..75
Love Them So Fully..77
No Competition...79
Stomped Up Bed of Lettuce.......................................80
No Space..82
I Am The Sea..83
I Started Talking To You The First Time........................84

HOW I WANT YOU
TO READ THIS BOOK

as a prayer.
as a wish.
as a secret.
as a nibbling on the ear.
as a note passing between
sweaty sixth-grade hands.
as a fogging window.
as thunder clap.
as comfort.
as communion.
as command.
as you want to,
as you need to.

SUBTLETIES

The way some flowers
curl up inside themselves.
Never touched. Never watered.
Like your shoulders concaving
at touch. Always nervous.
Always remembering.

HEAVY BLOOD

For girls who have never been touched right
a hand on the knee is a reason
for the instincts to click in.

Nails retract. Heads lower.
Eyes go numb on the floor.

Those girls' petals open without hesitation.
They know the always-changing rules.
How to hold their heads high
and suck in their stomachs.
How to scratch their pumping desire
of wanting *It*
from the inside.
How to be always glittering.
Always ready for the lights to flip on.
Always ready to be plucked.
Always.

Like they were trained to be.

PRIMAL DESIRE

You tell me that you are
interested in absolutes.
That what you need is tangibility,
rationality, something real to grab.
And I am a girl too dreamy,
too soft-mattered,
too much a shadow
for you.

But I want you to fuck me
senseless
because what logic
do we need to
undress each other-
fingernails in hair,
mouthes going limp,
bodies posed for an attack?

What reason is there to find
in the sweat on each other's
skin?

You are no formula.
You are a language I want
to moan in.

YOU LIKE THAT HUH

We are whispering in his rented room,
sharing whiskey beneath somebody else's sheets,
when he says,
I like it when you wear my shirts.
They make you look pure.

I laugh and take another swig
before getting up to use the bathroom.
There, bathed in yellow light,
I look at myself in the cracked mirror:
Little girl in an oversized shirt
with bare legs and a butchered tongue.

I should leave, I think.
I should go home, climb into bed,
try to forget this entire thing.

Instead, I climb back into his chest,
shape my body into one of his limbs,
and say,

Take off my cheeks,
suck on my eyes till they are hollowed out,
pull my pants down

and I'll moan how you like.
Give me a new name to wear,
a new face to study.
Help me out of this skin.
I so easily brand myself as yours
because I do not want to be mine.

I AM NOT THE SEA

I meet a boy who likes Bukowski and he wants to do brutal things to my body. He tells me he buys a bottle of whiskey whenever he gets one of his books and doesn't stop reading till he's gone through an entire pack of cigarettes. In his clean Los Angeles apartment, he blows smoke in my face and say, *He was the outcast king of L.A. Did you know that, huh?*

A new boy gives me a worn copy of *On the Road* and thinks he's being original. *We should explore the road together. Would you like that, baby?* Yes, I'd like that, I think. But he's drunk and imagining himself sixty years earlier, in the back of a bar, sweating to the sound of live bop. Still, I prefer him to the hungry boy that devoured my shirt and said, *You have a tattoo? What's it say? Mad to live? What, are you angry about living? Oh come on, I'm just kidding. Come here. Let me take off that bra.*

The next boy I kiss doesn't read. I ask him to come to a bookstore with me and he stays outside, sighing. He has no interest in words. He has no interest in me. I am thankful for him. For a few weeks, I am able to shed my habit of thinking obsessively and become a duller, rougher version of myself. But I dump him when my fingers start turning imaginary pages in my sleep.

I go on a date with a boy who knows I write. He calls himself a fan of mine and swears he's read every word I've put down. *You've got this voice that's very modern, but also so classic.* I nod, then choke on my water as he says, *I read you to fall asleep*. At night, I listen to him pant metaphors and compare my mouth to the sea. One day, he stumbles across my journal and finds nothing about himself in it. *You don't really love me, do you?* I shake my head. There is no use pretending anymore. He has read my poems about the boys I want to drown in me. Still, his goodbye leaves my hands covered in ink.

I try my best to become poetry. I take a bath and stain the water with black ink. I cry for people I have never met. I fashion my face into a pluckable flower. I shed self and skin, easily, readily. I widen my mouth, hoping waves will come. But no matter how hard I try, I am not the sea. I am a sunken ship that has drowned in everyone who touched me.

BABY DARLING HONEY

I only want him to tutor me in math
but he wants to feign sleep in me.
I want to finishing watching this movie
but he wants to get me a little closer.
Close enough that I become part of him:
a new limb, a second skin,
a womb for him to crawl back into.

He wants to gift me the same
baby darling honey
that has not stuck with sixteen others,
and I want to pretend
he can remember my name.

He cracks open a beer in his doorframe and says,
Here, baby, *Here, darling*, *Here, honey*,

and I feel all of the others he has invited
into his room lying on his bed.

They are all here,
taking the cold beer he offers,
letting him kiss their necks.
Together, in his mouth,
we are all *baby*, *darling*, and *honey*.

Lying next to them,

all I want to do is sleep,
but he picks at my neck
and asks to suck me clean.

But I only want to sink far enough
into the sea of myself
that I sputter and drown,
that I end up on my stomach

with no one to turn me over and say,
No! Is that you, baby darling honey?

HOW TO DISAPPEAR
(AND NEVER BE FOUND AGAIN)

The first things people always ask are, *why?*
And *how?*

But not me.

I don't want to do anything.
I don't want to be anything.

I want to disappear elegantly.
I want people to look for my goodbye note
and find smoke.

QUIET GAME STARTING NOW

Leaving parties without a word.
Leaving bars without telling my friends
where I'm going.
Chewing on *reckless* and *stupid* as I say,
Another shot of tequila, please.

I don't even like tequila.
I don't like throwing up in bed either,
but here I am,
with a bowl in my lap,
convulsing.

In the morning, I watch my brother
squeeze his smoothie
until bits of unblended fruit
drip onto his hand
and I wonder why my family walks
with resentment hooded around them.

Why I am still digging problems
that arose six years ago out of my thighs.

What I want is a womb of silence.
The quiet of a place where I don't exist.
I want to wrap myself in the stillness of it,

let it works its way into my ears

and paint over what's inside me.

Shhh.
Quiet game starting now.
Whoever breathes first loses.

TAKE YOUR TIME

Teach me how to be.
I am suffocating in me.

TODAY

I am taking large, *burn my belly*
gulps of coffee straight from the pot.
Today I am scratching my name into my thigh,
in hopes that I will not forget it by the time I go outside.
Today I am practicing not setting myself on fire.
Today I am the match.
Tomorrow I might be the smoke.
Today all sides of myself are swinging
their fists at each other in my stomach.
Tomorrow they may join together
in a prayer of forgiveness.
But today, I do not feel
like the resolved sound of settling.
Today the record of myself
is a trumpet's bare screech echoing into nothing.

RECLUSIVE

It is hard living
so deeply within myself.
There is nowhere to go
when I need a moment to think.

PATTER-MOUTHED

All of these art boys with their
big dreams of disappearing
tell me, *I'll be in this city someday.*

Nameless:
A small city that he walks through in photos
imagining himself
alone. Always alone.

He likes telling me all of the girls
he's fallen in love with as foreplay,
then touching me as he moans their names.

He likes panting *special* in my ear
and then leaving the taste of others on my lips
in case I get too comfortable.

Still I push my knees into his,
wet my lips a little
and say, *touch me.*

Touch me and don't think of them.
Touch me and tell me I feel good.

Touch me,
so for a bit I can forget
there isn't somewhere else you'd rather be.

BUT I THANK YOU FOR THE POEMS YOU GAVE ME

I wonder how we talked at all.
You are so many things I hate.
Your thin, off-white smile
hanging off your face like
an empty pack of gum.
Your drunken condescension.
The spittle crusted on your chin.
The packages of meat collected in your freezer.
Things you left to rot.
Like me.
Like me.

YOU KNOW THE WORD CONSENT

so I excuse you for drooling on my back
and texting me right after you leave
that I am a Thing You Want To Fuck.

All your friends say you are Progressive
All of mine say you are kind. Too kind.
They play your mixes in their cars
and make plans to visit you.
I laugh along with them
and dance in the front row at your shows
but say, *I'm sick*
so I do not have to say goodbye to you.

My friends say,
Why does this always happen to you?
How do you have so many stories like this?
It's him, it's him, it's HIM.
God, it's everyone, isn't it?

(What they don't say,
what I am sucking on in the silence is:
Maybe it's me.)

I laugh with them,
then place my hand over my mouth
to muffle my choking.

I don't like being this Thing
with dripping eyes and lips they
imagine fastening around their Cock
but I raise my arms, pout my lips,
and in they come, cursing: *I want to fuck you.*

You know the word *Consent*
But you don't use it with me.

LOOK

I don't care how Progressive
your friends,
my friends,
our friends
think you are.
Don't you dare send me
unwarranted dick pics again.

IS IT REALLY MY FAULT

My friends say that I have so many stories
of boys saying the wrong things to me.
So many complaints of drooling.
So many dreamy-eyed stories of them proposing *It*
as a question I can say no to.

My friends ask if I ever, you know,
thought that maybe it's uh, me?

(Ha ha ha. Good joke.
We all laugh together and then twiddle our tongues
around the truth that sits in our laps)

I tell them:
All of his text messages read,
Come on.
Don't make excuses.
Be. Down.

All of mine were blank accidents
or, *We'll see.*

I tell them:
He introduced himself with *I love you* and I,
being stupid being bored
being so used to this
that I no longer interact

I just type a reply, hit send,
and wait for the next pawn to hatch
gave him my number when he asked.

I tell them:
I'm stupid I'm bored
I am so used to this
that I no longer see it
as anything new.

All their faces become the same,
with a single mouth of thirst
and one great proposition of *It*
they do not have to finish spitting out
before I nod.

I tell them:
Yes. I have thought about
whether or not it was me.
But what is my solution?
Death? Bitterness? Killing of my Kind Mouth?

Should I slice off my Smile and replace it with a
Stab Wound that says,
I have heard this all before?

What would it change?
I tell them:
what they want to hear.

My friends. These men.
And still, the silence sticks
to my mouth like a question
I was never really given a chance
to say *no* to.

AN OFFERING

I didn't just want you to fuck me,
I wanted you to love me.

But I didn't know what
to convince you with
besides my body.

HAND-ME-DOWN RAG

All the ones who touched me
but refused to have me.
Who asked me to sleep in their bed
but not talk to them
when their friends were around.

I mourn them.
Not for the loss of them.
But for what they took.

For being introduced to my body
as a bouquet of petals
and leaving it as a pile of stems-
clipped
undesirable
unwanted.

THE DUST ON THIS POEM COULD CHOKE YOU

I am shaking on the ground in my bedroom,
realizing that it is two years until
I turn the age you wanted to marry me.
I am using the candles on my
twenty-first birthday cake to burn my knees.
I am in the front row at a show,
knowing that if I heard this song two years ago,
I would have thought about you.

Thinking about you takes effort now.
You no longer pour out when I open my mouth.
These days, if I want to bleed you out,
I have to grab a knife.

I am in the doctor's office,
refusing to quiver when she asks me if I'm okay.
I am biting down on my lip until I taste rust
when she mentions putting me on antidepressants.
I am figuring out which parts of my personality
are mine and which ones I created to please you.
I am getting better, I swear.

I am burning every poem with your name in it.
But I am still holding onto
some of the letters you wrote me.

I tell myself I'm not sentimental.
I tell myself it's because
I am afraid of forgetting the early warning signs.

I'm not sentimental.
I'm just afraid of throwing every burning thought
I have about you into the trash
and starting a fire.

YOUR TYPE

That's what you like in a girl: cute and sad,
with enough disorders that you could
count them to fall asleep.
The kind you can show off at parties
as the latest broken thing you fixed.

But where will you hang your awards
for loving someone
who can't walk in a straight line
without being supported?
Is there room next to your
collection of glasses you shattered
by holding too tightly?

The blood on your hands
does not make you a martyr.
Do not curse when your hammers
do nothing but scar.
Do not use your words
to remind her that everybody else
would have left by now.

If she could speak, she would tell you:
You think it's beautiful to love somebody
as light as me,
but you don't know how heavy I had to be
to become this empty.

YOU WERE AN ILLNESS
I BARELY BEAT

Here is a list of reasons we should have quit each other long before we did:

Because, while driving in the car with you, I looked at bridges and wondered how big of a splash I would make if I hit the water below them. Because you told me I was gross when I spit on the page that said *stain this*. Because you never questioned what I was thinking about when I went silent for hours in the thrift store. Because I didn't think you'd care that I was wishing it was big enough for me to get permanently lost in.

Because I wrote down what made me sad and all of them were things you told me about myself. Because my breaking point was making a list of reasons I should leave and reasons I should stay, even though I already knew which side would be longer. Because I wrote, in clear sober letters, that I didn't think kisses could get me by anymore.

Because whenever I get low, I hear your voice in my head listing all of the things about me that will never be good enough. Because you roared at me (that is the only way I can describe it, your teeth were bared and your eyes grew hot right then) and I cannot shake the image of me afterwards, stumbling away, blinded by tears, and feeling so incredibly lonely that my bones still shake just thinking about it.

Because, by the end, I felt like I should hate myself to have something in common with you. Because I have to resist pounding my pillow and screaming that you were supposed to be one of the good ones. Because I accepted you telling me that I always victimize myself and began to hate the tears in my eyes and the stupid way I'd sit in the corner, picking at scabs and trying so hard to win you back each time we fought. Because I stabbed a painting of mine in a fit of self-hate and because it had been a gift for you, you got mad and took it as a sign that I did not love you, instead of asking me what was wrong.

Because when I desperately asked you to please just hide the bottle of pills in the bathroom from me, I acted like I was asking a stranger for a favor, not like I was confessing that I could not stop thinking about walking the thirty steps to the bathroom, turning on the shower, and letting steam fill the room until somebody realized I had collapsed on the floor long ago.

THE THOUGHT OF YOU

I'm sorry that
I only called after
drinking six cups of coffee,
but something about shaking
always reminds me of you.

I PRACTICE DEATH
TO FORGET YOU

I do all the things you used to hate.
I go to bed without dinner and become air.
I give up reading. I give up Leonard Cohen.
I never eat another plate of scrambled eggs.
I leave Canada.
I let go of the softness that drew you to me.
My speech sharpens. My teeth turn to fangs.
This is what it takes to survive.
I do what it takes to forget you,
and by the end,
have more bruises than I started with,
but I can finally look at a sunset
and not feel anything at all.

FLANK OF MEAT COOKED UP

My body:
Is my body.

My body.
Is my body. Is my body.
Is my body. Is my body.
Is my body is my body.

My body.
Is mine.

So why
does it feel
like a branded piece
of yours?

MAKE IT REAL

I am wholly myself.
Before I am a piece of anybody else.

JUST SO IT'S CLEAR

You don't know how to be touched.
You don't know how to be loved.
You are lonely and push away
anybody who tries to get close.

You are a ship going under
because you cannot stop
pouring water onto your hull.
And I am the bucket that will never be
big enough to hold all of the drowning
in you.

SALT

She does not come to you
with a mouthful of salt by chance.

She was taught
to like it when he calls her a *bitch*.
Taught to stay still when he puts his hands
around her neck tight enough to bruise.

Now when he whispers
about pushing her to the ground
and slapping her across the face,
she moans a little.

So when you kiss her,
do so full of tongue and easy softness.

Pant her name. Kiss her neck.
Brush your finger over the dry flakes
on her bottom lip.

Run them along your teeth.
Taste how they came to her.

Taste how breaking her rocks
into easily digestible flakes
was something she was taught.

HE IS A SONG I HAVE STUCK IN MY HEAD

I look at photos of your ex
and imagine the two of you at fifteen.
I see the light on your braces
as you tried to shape yourself
into his version of beautiful.
You, all burnt hair and too-full Love
and Him, a set of restrictions
you tried to learn before they were taught to you.

Now he is a dirty body of water.
A sullied stream
(with half-washed clothes still floating down him.)
A song you sing sometimes
in-front of all your friends.

At your band's first show,
I listen to you sing about Him and think,
I hate these songs we write
about our failures-
the water-marked pains that we keep
drowning in-
and how they always get stuck in my head.

PURITY IS A BARBED-WIRE FENCE SHOUTING KEEP OUT

Look,
you are a holy ocean
into which they plunge.

We can all tell you hold too many
untouched continents to count.
We have our flags ready,
hoping that you will let
one of us claim you.

You ring in our ears,
you tangle our vocal chords.
We sing you in our sleep.

But you contain so much of
what we want that we threaten
to drain you completely.

So, I tell you this:
Keep your hills green,
your lakes full of fish,
your sunsets unphotographed.
When we come by the shipload,
turn us away.

We will only mark you,
then leave.
And you deserve so much more
than our footprints on you.

SEX WITH YOU

is boring sex
Like: I could be
painting my nails right now
or checking my email
or scraping gum off my shoe.

Sex without love
is a flower-filled vase sitting dusty
in the kitchen
and I am tired
of seeking others to water
what is not wilting.

With my hands in-between
my legs, I pluck
until the warmth
waters itself.

PUT PRESSURE ON A WOUND TO STOP IT FROM BLEEDING

Your tongue is working my thighs
Giving them massage more than pleasure
when you say,
I want you to be my woman.

Your woman.
You kiss my ear
and leave the request there.

I am a woman possessed
A woman unsatisfied
A spell-casting woman
clucking her tongue
as she recites your name.
An assertive woman
A longing woman,
dancing in shapes with you
when you are not there.

A learning woman.
A womb of a woman,
pregnant with selves.
A woman that is so many women.

But your woman?
Even with my back arched
and hair matted with your sweat
I do not like the sound of it.

THE WOMEN WIDOWED
TO THEMSELVES

Women who fuck often but rarely go on dates.
Past and Present Women,
laughing out different version of themselves.

Your mother calls them
Disgusting Women,
not realizing whom she is talking to.

Branded as the Easy Women,
their bodies a game,
their flirtations a strategy.

Call *checkmate*
with your hand in their mouths.
Call *checkmate*
until they bite at your finger
and lick a little at the blood.

TRAINED SILENCE
After Angel Nafis

Good Girl goes to party and counts her drinks.
Good Girl never drinks too much.

Good Girl doesn't call you out on your jokes.
Good girl smiles nervously in hopes that you like her.

Good Girl makes fun of herself before you can.
Good Girl swallows your insults
and says you're a good guy.

Good Girl plays dead when you kiss her.
Good Girl wakes up covered in you
and is too drunk and too sweet
to push you off.

Good Girl swallows her anger
and untangles your apology.
Good Girl knows you didn't mean it.
Good Girl knows you'd never do that conscious.

Good Girl, a stream you sullied.
Good Girl, so sick of being good.
So sick of kindness that is really trained silence.

Good Girl becoming river current.

Good Girl becoming wave.
Good Girl, ready to drown
the next hand that dives into her uninvited.

Good Girl.
Come take a dip in her.
I dare you.

CAN'T KEEP UP

The heart wants
what it wants

But sometimes my heart wants
things I cannot give it:
A fresh start
A new self
A place to be emptied

Sometimes my heart wants things
I have to grab from its hands and say,
No! Put that down!

Like, knives or pills
or scissors I could
cut out pieces of my eyelids with

Sometimes my heart wants everything
and must be sat down and told
to be happy with what it has.

BIRTHDAY CAKE

Do you know what it is like
to have poems kicking inside of you?
Making bruises on your throat
Putting their hands around your bones
and saying, *Write me! Write me!*
Tell others what you are too afraid
to even think about.

Do you know what it is like
to swallow so much Loneliness
that it stains everything you taste?

Like a burned tongue that never heals.
Like your own mother watching you
punch yourself repeatedly in the face
then telling you that you are too old
to be so *angsty*.

It is like five hundred and fifty three
candles burned into a birthday cake.
Each counting a time
you thought you would not live.
That you could not live.
Not like this. Not anymore.

AN APOLOGY TO MY BODY

I am sorry for filling you with beer and bad thoughts
and then asking you why you shook.
I am sorry for pinching you, for hitting you,
for bruising the thin-skinned parts of you.
I am sorry for the names I called you
when we were fighting.
You are not ugly.
You are not useless.
You would not be better off gone.

I'm sorry for almost throwing you into the street
because my hurt was too much for me.
I'm sorry for carving my fingernails
into your thigh and then
resenting the way people asked,
How'd that happen?

I'm sorry for plucking you
and nicking your calves with drugstore razors.
I'm sorry I let people see you in the moonlight.
They didn't deserve to know
the color of your hips like I do.
I'm sorry for leaving you convulsing
over a toilet bowl because of some boy.

I'm sorry that this apology is ten years too late.

I'm sorry that it will probably come again.
I'm sorry that I do not treat anybody else
 as poorly as I have treated you.
I'm sorry that I am constantly
learning how to love you,
when you have never once doubted
how you feel about me.
I'm sorry in ways I have
not yet learned to communicate.

CAN YOU TASTE THE SELF-LOATHING IN THIS POEM

You insult me
as if the worst names
haven't come out of my
own mouth before.
But you could never
hate me as much as I
once hated myself.

Go ahead,
keep your tongue
heavy. I have already
survived the worst.

THE JOY OF BEING ALIVE

All of a sudden
I miss everyone
even the ones
who are not gone
yet.

HOW CAN YOU HAUNT ME
IF YOU'RE STILL HERE

I apologize for not knowing how
to talk to you anymore.
I try to shape my lips
into the neck of a bottle
so you will pour your secrets
into me with ease,
but choke on memories of you
throwing up whiskey on school nights.

Lately, I have put myself to sleep
by counting all of the times
I could have been more for you.
But sharing a bed with my failures
only leaves me with a pounding headache
in the morning.

All I have to show for trying
to love your ghost
are arms outstretched to air,
and yet, I'd rather you haunt me than say *goodbye*.

IT'S LIKE A POEM I KEEP WRITING

Loneliness like a sore
on the inside of your cheek.
You tongue at it and
a little blood drips out
and ah, there it is,
the taste of familiarity.
Like scratching without an itch.
Like cause without effect
except: the inability to articulate,
to sleep soundly,
to communicate
comfortably.
Like emotion without motive.

I have no motives,
only this uncut fingernail
scrscrscratching that I cannot itch.
Loneliness is a scratchy tune
on a radio show
three towns down.
Through the static
you make out the words:

You create something to miss
to remind yourself that you exist.

AS SOON AS I FORGET
I AM REMINDED AGAIN

I will
not get sad.
I will not get sad.
I will shed no tears,
feel no rain,
taste no rust

for things that were always going
to be brief.

YOUR HEART IS THE SIZE OF A FIST BECAUSE YOU NEED IT TO FIGHT

My mother told me that it's time to stop
worrying about who I am
and time to start worrying about money.

I wonder if everyone is sat down
and forced to give up their heart.
If killing it is a thought-out, calculated decision.

Are some more wrinkled
because they put up a bigger fight?

If so, my face will look like a
one-line painting by the end,
with new lines popping up every minute,
because I will never stop spitting up
the passion in my throat.

HOT SUN THROUGH MY JEANS

I contain
everything I have done
and everyone I have been
in this bursting skin.

I SING THE SONG OF MYSELF

Bleeding poetry and thinking
nothing of the consequences.
I let Want speak to me
in a steady breath
and listen to it openly.
I am with Whitman,
singing the song of
myself until the notes
are memorized.

I group whatever pieces of themselves
others give me into something I call *me*.
Every day, I am relearning
the tune of myself.

Memory says,
*You have done this dance
so many times before*

And I respond,
I will do this dance inside
as many different cities,
bodies, and seasons as I can.

I am not looking to be narrow
in mind, experience, or belief.
Nor contained in *girl, sister*,

ex-, *lover*, *woman*, or *friend*.

I will die a verb,
a force, a thing that has
bled out so many names
that no noun can hold it.

PULLING FEATHERS

He was all slapped red cheeks and too-short jeans.
I kissed him until his mother came home
and laughed at our backwards sweaters
and lack of breath.

He was all *pick you up at eight*,
see him at ten.
Loving him was a wait-
waiting for his car to pull up,
waiting for his call,
waiting for him to feel the same.
I thought he was saying *I love you too*
when he talked about knee highs and
his parents going out of town,
but all he was saying was *I want to fuck you.*

He was all innocent curls and '60s rock-
a child that had not outgrown rebellion.
My thighs were another way to stick it to their parents
who, upon seeing us sucking the marrow
out of each other,
winked and presented me with my very own
daughter in law nickname. Poor thing.
The last thing they wanted was the hickey
I left on their neck to spell *forever*.

He was all timid shakes and coffee breaks,
with never a penny in his pocket.
A season with him was drunken insomnia
and game shows.

Beautiful and full of late-night
loneliness, but sad, so sad. His last text read:
The birds may know about the heaven
we look for with ladders,
but I'll never know unless I jump.

I am all scars and broken parts,
a collapsed choo choo train that ran out
of steam months ago.

Choo choo, I say.
If you're the one pulling feathers
out of your spine, I've been looking for you.

WHEN YOUR HEART BREAKS GET UP AND STOMP ON IT

Let's fall in love like
our parents never taught us to
confuse comfort and complacency.
Like we aren't picking glass from our soles.
Like we have more to offer each other
than bouquets of fears.
Let's fall in love like we're sixteen-
untouched, blushing,
not yet knowing that
we are capable of cutting someone open.
Let's fall in love with our
heels in our mouths.
Like we haven't done this before.
Let's fall in love like that's it.
Like we never had a choice.

SEND THIS TO YOUR VALENTINE

I want you to love me, hard.
Whatever that means.

Love me like it's the last thing
you're going to do.
Love me like I am a burning building
and your cat is trapped in me.
Love me, I've heard all your
embarrassing bad stories
and still want to stay up talking.

I've got no time for lukewarm love
or *rather be sleeping* sex.
No time for any love that isn't
pushing me out a window,
shattering glass
and shouting, *Jump! Jump! Jump!*

No time.

I want to burn my hands on you,
choke on too much of you,
come up sputtering and use my
first gasp of air to say,

I'm going back down.

MADE UP IN YOUR MAKE-UP

I think I have a crush on
the person I could be with you.
A lighter me,
A more *me* me.

Wearing light
and licking it from your skin
Trading cracked open heads
like drops passed between streams.

I want to be the drink
you swish around your teeth.

I want to empty myself
and be refilled
with water-marked pieces of you.

THE SLIVERED WALKS

I want you to undress me
to the sound
of all of your defenses
collapsing.

NEW SELF SAME CITY

I.
We were people who loved each other once.
How nice to rub it off.
To wipe it from our tongues.
To acknowledge our love
existing outside of us.
A relic we outgrew.

We pump our elbows at it.
Make references to it. Laugh and blush about it.

How nice it feels to try on old selves
like a coat in the fitting room.
To examine aspects of yourself you let go
in a three-way mirror
and not feel regretful
for shrugging yourself clean of them.

II.
How nice it is to say his name in this town.
I hold its newness inside of me-
a small pearl of warmth, a place to hide in,
a reminder of the Present-
When I leave bars early,
surrounded by groups of former friends,
I wrap it around me.

Here
I whisper his name
until every self I am
and have been
sings along.

LOVE THEM SO FULLY

Falling in love when you thought
you never would again,
when you thought you had your chance
and that was it, feels weird.
So what.
Suck on it. Swish it around your mouth.
Does it taste like anything you've swallowed before?
Go ahead, spit it up if you have to.
Drink too much of it too quickly
and send yourself running to the bathroom.
Make bold plans too soon, too fast.
A few months in, decide to move in together,
despite telling yourself you would never move in
with anyone you loved again.

So what so what so what.
Regret is not a universal word.
Did you learn anything,
in your years of practicing non-love?
Did sucking on the lonely idea
of never finding love again
teach you about the taste of it?

Hard lover, soft lover,
lover so in love with
the idea of love that they get sick on it.

Lover with a garden so full
that blossoms spurt out of their mouth
whenever they open it.

Love them like this:
By picking them.
By plucking them.
By giving yourself so fully
that petals grow into them.

NO COMPETITION

Sometimes when I look at you
I almost say his name,
the way you accidentally said her name
while telling me how important I was.

It scares me,
these pasts we keep inside of ourselves.
These experiences we carry
that neither of us can touch.

I want to love you deeper
than anyone has.
And yet I hate
the way you tell me
you are not attracted to her anymore.
These words we offer to
erase all past,
in hopes that we each feel loved.

Forget loving deeper.
I want what was to teach me
how to love you deeply.
This is no competition.
This is only a promise
that I will care about you
for all the people you
have been and will be.
For the person you are.

STOMPED UP BED OF LETTUCE

The last month of your probation
I think about something going wrong
Anything
and you being shuttered away in steel.

I begin to count down the days
The minutes
until your court date
I learn the weight of Time
(It is my 140 lbs. collapsed against your bathroom sink)
The sound of it
(It is any car that stops for too long)
(It is a siren swooping around a corner)
I tell myself, there are lovers separated by wars
By natural disasters by borders
and they all know the weight of Time
much clearer than I do

I know Time as a promise
I have not had to make yet
A promise to love you even if it is
fear wrapped around my neck
every time a car drives by.
Even if driving through downtown
leaves me breathless
because of all its neon lights.

I promise:
I will keep your side of the bed warm
until you get back.

NO SPACE

The money is running out
and I'm scared.
What felt like a lot is not a lot.
We have three blankets,
a shelf full of toys
you found in abandoned homes,
and too many stolen markers.

This is everything we own.
Some people have homes full of things.
Some people have objects to fill every corner.

Our room is all space,
but when we look at each other,
we fill it.
There is no space big enough
for how I feel about you.

I AM THE SEA

It is different with you.
That is so much a cliche
that I could chew it up
and all you would see
would be dust.

But it's true.
It is different.
With you.
Sweeter. Easier.

With more nervous shaking
thinking about you,
and for what?

You want me.
I know that you want me
because the stickiness of me
coated you and you said,

Submerge me.
I want to be drowned in you.

I STARTED TALKING TO YOU THE FIRST TIME I PICKED UP A PEN

I always wondered
who these poems
were about,
but then I
met you.

ACKNOWLEDGMENTS

I have enough *thank you*s to fill a book, a new book, but:

Thank you to my family for keeping my bedroom door closed when I said I was writing poems. To Kevin for teaching me how to pick gravel out of skinned knees. To Caroline for her unfailing strength. To my mother for showing me the weight shoulders can carry.

To Clementine for her poems and direction. To Kiki for all the work she does. To Meggie, Caitlyn, and the other young writers who have supported me for years.

To Robi, Mindy, Jamie, Ben, Jo, Jancie, Carly, Nature, Kasey, Matt Bear, and Cheyenne for giving *family* a larger meaning to me.

To the Che Cafe for giving me a momentary home.

To Matt, for seeing the pieces of myself I try to hide and not looking away. So much of this is for you.

PREVIOUSLY PUBLISHED

"The Dust On This Poem Could Choke You" was originally published in *The Fem Literary Magazine* in 2014.

"An Apology to My Body" was originally published in the short collection, *bigger bolder less pathetic.*

ABOUT THE AUTHOR

Lora Mathis is a poet and photographer who grew up hopping between San Diego and Montreal. Right now, home has a question mark after it. She is the Senior Manager of Art for *Persephone's Daughters* and has had her creative work published in *Words Dance*, *Lumen Magazine*, *The Fem*, and *Adbusters*. She writes to place herself.

Where Are You Press

Printed in Great Britain
by Amazon.co.uk, Ltd.,
Marston Gate.